undersleep

undersleep
julie doxsee

Octopus Books
Lincoln, Nebraska
2008

OCTOPUS
BOOKS

ISBN 13: 978-0-9801938-0-0
ISBN 10: 0-9801938-0-x

Cover art by Jake Gillespie
www.jakegillespie.com

Cover design by Samuel B. Rapien
www.imightbealright.com

Printed in the United States

Published by Octopus Books
Lincoln, NE
www.octopusbooks.net

Acknowledgments

Poems in this manuscript have been published in the following journals: *Good Foot*; *The Bedazzler*; *Aufgabe*; *LIT Magazine*; *La Petite Zine*; *H_NGM_N*; *Octopus*; *Spork Magazine*; *Conduit*; *Action, Yes*; *Tarpaulin Sky*; *Fourteen Hills*; *Shampoo*; *Typo*; and *Eratio Postmodern Poetry*.

Selected poems have been published as the chapbook *You Will Build a City Out of Rags* (Whole Coconut Chapbook Series).

undersleep

YOUR DRY-EYE CURSE

Because that cloud
I'm pointing to has been raining on my town
six years straight

it's not the weight of the
house affecting
my disappearance into
mud. You'd
sink when the part of
our body that is legs
takes charge.

YOU WILL BUILD A CITY OUT OF RAGS

Silence, tall as a young boy
interested in flight sewing the
scents of the lower branches

neither to his nose nor
over the leaves themselves.
Tunnels in the tinier heart find

air pleasing & so naked.

Electric currents weave one thread

nine times throughout
blurs & tones

retained from a game of
yard-nymph. You will swell
from every danger boiling.

I will fracture
each outer-space
radio with potlatch.

Ghastly & ornamental.

These are undulations
tiptoeing the inches.

Lie down diagonally
until I leave dimples
in your shave.

Young enough to feed each

other a finger, warmth starts

under the throat

then migrates

so we see it

over our heads.

Weather is an

igloo of gray. When I
languish in a pile of ice, I
laze nice out of its stiffness.

Because. Because the city
turns watery with
lightning.

LIKE A TRUNK

I wake the torso of
a clone

against the snore
you shake

& pull out the drill
& make a quick

treehouse to keep.

CONTINUUM

Attribute the color of

        blue trees to
        the blue bird

atrophying in your skull.

        I negotiate rib
        and low lamp

with the backdrop of

        ornaments
        swinging gently

near your head.   Envy me

        because
        I'm not

ghostly. Along the scrim,

        you close in
        on the slow

hand blackening electricity,

        wearing you
        as a night light.

ON YESTERDAY'S STATUE

The girl swam downstream

to the desert, found you
asleep as a spider.

One type of word
bled through

the undeclared
crawl, beautiful because.

Off in the jungle

a tickle of
arms became

the sound
of geese who

bathe close
to humans & look deep

into our eyes.

LIMITED TO OUTLYING VISIONS

Leaning is a test

unsuitable for

lungs, touchable & puffed. The

triangle of sky teeters

murk from

eventual seas. I meet you in the

bed of pearls,

devoured blood

hitting the dead heart. Robot birds

dig bark with metal

beaks when

we oust ourselves from the

standstill.

Songs open up

above the little suns

there, pre-keening

for planets not yet fallen.

RELEASE OF UNDERGROUND GRAY

Out of 1000
tiny vapors, a flare
in the right corner

of the frame dims
the eye people tap,
each pearl-tipped

flower crowding
wherever
rain pounds

exteriors into mud.

ROCK ERODES A LIFESPAN

Clouds take blue from *could*. Could be clouds are the rind of a ripe sky.

An outside eye holds all lakes and oceans in one mirror.

The body casts an object onto its shadow two or three times. An eclipse lives nowhere then wrestles awake. Nighttime can't stretch darkness when the moon is engulfed by noise.

Hold a piece of dust at arm's length and watch its two-dimensional twin burn at noon. Gray stranger, make your gray a happier thing. Nighttime erases as it grows over the eye.

The earth's rind forms an outer layer where fruit sprouts. Leaves detach from xylem after sucking skin. A rock conducts its upside-down mountain.

Discovery invites the collapse of something high. Sky. Paradise. Wing-pilot. Echelon. Uncrater holding bits of ground.

Uncover the rock. Fig leaves fall off and die, but there are more fig leaves in a grove you'll visit naked. Forget leaves & now branch & trunk.

Meteors orbit other rocks as a planet orbits skin after one magical boom.

I have a memory of this: day is a death-form with painted edges. Movement cycles above the rock. Before you doorbell, water-blast yourself a shape to wriggle around in.

The base is sensitive to youch. Touch. An avalanche blots the sun, erosion explodes light through the eye or tongue.

Every morning at sunrise the same Mount Fuji finds a canvas and so exists no more. Algorithms float the world into. Paradise is dead hope for a zigzag trance. There is no such thing as the plateau-outside-the-self smelling rose bouquets.

Mountains dwarf the fig leaf an orgasm launched to the roadside. We no longer subtract space from time or time from space.

There is by sun on the other side of night, unseen. Moon is sun's meridian spy, her blue pornography stomached in half-twilight by shady actors. A mountain is an uncompleted dream with steep sides you slick up your hands on. My.

The mountain is a world with its own weather. Windows crack only when the ingénue twirls her umbrella toward the fountain. Desire is the MORE we invent and store for the winter in shoe boxes.

Film runs out. The earth is not a building. It is paper born in the woods & hacked into rectangles children flip through. The horizon is one border. But the edge is convex per Christopher Columbus whose halo shines down from outer-space like a star you pointed to & never saw fall.

THE DEEP SHADOW LIFE OF YOUR COUSIN

is

counter-

feiting

the sound of

weeds

after

osmosis,

of hands

full of petals

recently shook.

MAGNETIC STRIPS

When they brought
the pots & pans

you banged
out of your body

it took seven
humans to carry

what came out
of your throat.

I couldn't drink

a fishbowl of
salt after that;

my mouth was
down the street

stuck shut.

MOTION SONG

Singular
reality hosts

an idiot horseman

while the object
surpasses its own

dark limit.
Make believe is

secretly
make believe.

Yesterday
is a jet-streak

until thin vapors

lose last month's
moon.

SLEEP IN WITH STILL-LIFE

Wake up under the
doorframe today, he says, while

eating the final orange slice.
Doorframe, he repeats.

LANDSCAPE

Your people wander from the ceiling to
     turn knobs

sideways from a split-in-two
       chair. The door leads safely to horizontal air

you can eat or climb on. Air will cube itself
       without the need for air-cube trays according to
       your people.

I feel the uncold air deep
      freeze as it lands

near your feet. By the look on your face
      I feel the weather

soak walls. You
      take the waterfall from its

hideaway and fold it
      for storage.

ACHILLES

Achilles on the moor
sees a rash of footprints

followed by a

collage of peafowl.

Not so pinheaded
to count

flaws of the

wing. One only. Out of
eighty birds.

Cavalry, bring

out your ponies for little old
me. Pie cools, falcons loop-to-loop

either with or against the thrust.

TAKING PICTURES OF EVERYTHING

Telescopic rail station, a
hello on the door holds

the metal lasso we've
looked around for for

ages. Say as we trap it it
saturates & leaks through

twisted glass or dangles into
winter never freezing

or taking an eye out
with its never-speared finger.

THE SMALL FACTORIES OF MORNING

Everybody has
a moonbeam

under the covers.
Of the dozen

midnight faces
none hold

the rain cupped.

THE ONE WHO SWALLOWED FALCONS

In the night a hard beak
speaks your preference

for live mice via
puppet

throat, embossed wings
in a swan dive under your

collar. I feel the black
eye peek through your mouth, that mouse-nest
hair of mine eyed for signs of scampering.

I sleep well-covered by pillows.

In the day you talk falcon talk.

Ordinarily I would

fear the talons of a
killer, tongue of the eye

aligned with the flesh of my
head. You drove me double,

stuffed me
into a backpack

already full of me.

LAVISH DESCENTS

Believe in

lavish descents, he says, as he
un-names a room full of

cats, attaching a
leash to each small throat.

MY WINTER FILM

Anthony is a good
name for a
whale.

And presto, the ink
forms indelible
obscenities

addressed to mortals.
Out in the
mud, we

sweet-talk footage
shot with a
broken zoom

until it looks
rained on.

SUBLIMITY

The whisper
crosses the

room then turns to
cloud.

*

Possibility is an oafish
shush

in a tiny
chirp.

PERIMETER A

Let me kill the Paradise around the wall as I walk it. Pregnant-minded. An entrance is edged in mountain shade.

Let me stun invention to bewildered stares as you dig the soft grave. Gate the stars. Disguise the soft grave. Shadows & dust take the wind up up & away. The tender nape of the neck is shocked by electric fingerprints. Teeth shift shape to tender the animal breath.

Let me remember shadows buried around the wall and watered, every twilight, by big-boned children. No longer does the mouth exist. English breaks from the lower gut. Inner inhabitants meet versions of themselves in chambers dug by small fingers. Still wet. Scent of far burnt particles. This echo is driven by six white horses. This echo is the shrill loss I look in the face as it scrapes my knee, gone before blood beads. The woman waits at the gate with dirty lambs around her feet.

PERIMETER B

It takes 3 weeks to eat the poem. Three weeks of long mornings and coffee hidden under the table where banshees play jacks for big money. Nobody knows. The act.

Twilit foliage dries as vines die in a ravine. A girl gathers rocks and piles them on her belly.

A past rips in half, one side of itself wounded at the split, umbilical eyes still holding. As the afternoon passes it shrinks to a speck in the clouds.

When eyes meet they don't touch. The eye never ages distance. Anyone could be gazing directly at you from the stratosphere. Now. Anyone is gone.

GATE C

Dry weeds are not handholds. Security ripped earlier from root,
loose rocks eroding from foot, foothills stung by heavy moon.

When I shuffle the ledge, my skin in the night opens. When
I tiptoe over the arch in the sky, my skin closes and my bones
open. All the way up. The blood on the rock is invisible on
a clear night such as this one. Stars are objectless light sucked
from black holes. There is nothing here therefore. No base. No
perimeter. No below. Between songs I speak like a five-year-old
familiar with real angels. My feet are electronic bridges, eroding,
meant to wake me.

PERIPHERAL

Paradise is not a thing to keep.

Shadows are little nighttimes
for pronouncing

night's hymn.

*

Night's hymn
cannot contain

doses of
Paradise. Sleep

is a movement through *not*.

*

Undersleep thickens want as it prods.

Make the proper substitutions above.

MIRAGE

If the brick holds

water, mortar
is likely to

change tidy cubes
to footprints.

HISTORY SUGGESTS A SQUALL

What could smooth the

clouds as clouds
mix up airplanes.

A hound
laps rain puddle.

You play blackjack
in my longest

naked dream.
One arrow hunts

a yard for
smooth twigs but there

are no such things.

POND

Thereafter she
left her dress

wriggling free.
A boy's dog

sniffed it out
and drew legs

in the sand.
Later on

a turtle
nestled up

under the skirt,
where little high-

ways of murk
bled through blue

linen. You.
Even you set

a footprint each
year near

her imprint.

TINY TRICKS OF SUBSTANCE

butt up to

howls
animated by horns.

A Sunday depends

on the moon's
metaphor,

not on the object's

spongy surface.

Who invented the
weight of. Gravity.

Wind. The absence of

halo. Hail.

TWIST GENTLY AS YOU HUNT

unless the
nut &
apple still-life

is kicked over
by the hooves
of wayward

buffalo.
Fight the
avalanche.

TREADABLE SKY

Welcome, flying
meteorite,

ask for whatever
you might

inhale.

The tiger will
eat raw falcons,

wash them down
with moat

water.

SONG FOR ONE VIOLIN

The heart
I hear

matches
road gloss

with no sound.
Attention to

blurs will provide
the ear

you need
to wind

your way
to the other side.

FACADE

The arrow
u-turns

to an island
full of huts

broken over
your knee.

The heart
lumbers slow

collisions
with horrible

red ants.
The sand

would be real
unless gunshots

went off &
came back

from the mirage
every minute

or two.

ARBORETUM

Kill the
story
of an
avalanche

attendant
to its
deadly
uproar.

Deciduous
trees
cling
to rock,

bored with
aphids
nibbling
pieces of

branch.

ROPED-OFF GRAVITY

A glint of blue

butterflies its way
across the

throats of seven
children.

A wheel is

the forwardness
we thought

emerged only as
accidental

tongues.

FIGURES

A thickening.

It is full of cups and stops a cup. It has long fingers, unable to make bones. It debates while kindness droops. It walks a dog while people stare. It loses car keys. It hits the ceiling with its head. It is full and biteable. It whelms, it wells. It curls over with magnet eyes.

An expectation.

It is fermented. It is a dry candle and a spill of roast fish. It howls and chokes on spit. It sleeps and forgets easily and is trapped in a snow bank. It has money, no pockets. It screams when a taxi whizzes. It splashes and turns toward knolls. It forgets.

A vacancy.

It hates a refrigerator full of cheap beer. It hates rice. It is a saucepan with beads of water. It is a TV show on a stilted TV. It is a glance dumped onto the carpet. It is an arm span, a finger span, a running with air.

An until.

It is a native in the jail. It is a death. It is a future and a bigfoot.
It is branded on the flank. Mountains hang from above. It grows
mold to be eaten, then has no mold at all. It has a heartbeat, but
no warm head to pat. It is a thick temple of clichés and touches,
but goes away untouched.

A generation.

It is five spaceships in the noon light. It had lunch with Cher
once. *Thee* Cher. It is a study of ice cubes and cold fusion.
It wears only beige. It is too loud and rides a broken bicycle.
Suddenly it says *fuck* at the same time each evening. It sips and
clicks through a filmstrip.

A turmoil.

It is a small place in the wall in which aphids hide. It is a notch,
but you shouldn't poke it. It is a chemical & grows nice tomatoes.
It is a buzzing. It forgets to button up and makes off with a faux
silk tapestry. It is a fisherwoman.

An hour.

It is tidy with stringy legs. It tastes like a twisted lime, not a dried lime. It is a grandfather minding the chicken coop. It is saggy—tidy and saggy both. It is a barbell floating in the harbor. It eats sardines, nothing expensive.

DISFIGURES

A shampoo.

A scattering of nine days afraid of blackened tubs. A shampoo is afraid of dark fireflies and orange t-shirts in the rain. A shampoo is a very short building.

A teapot.

A teapot's hands are curly hard hands with very clean knuckles. A teapot whistles as strangers peep.

A fence & an arrow.

Behind the shed is a pile of wheat from long long ago.

A ballet record.

A ballet record will become GOD if the ballet record has a strong light.

A portrait of red devils.

A friend deserves a birthday present and a few small notches to stomp. A friend deserves a bridesmaid's foot. A friend deserves to twirl.

0

Brown vapor
from the full loose
mouth.

RIGHT ARM

In the
yellow flaps

of door
revolving

clean out of the
sleep wiped

from circling

"A" words:

Anvil. Ardor.
Also. A

"love of god"
sand dune is topped

with a bracelet and a
barbell.

There is no one in sight.

The
left-handed one
walked, see,

but never near the dune.

ICE SHAPES

A mercury spill
follows you, spelling
between figure 8s:

the large cloud
fell from the wall
with sugar-water before

leaping to the magnet
wall. A curl of my
pillow-head-you

goes upsidedown
with a vase of orchids
as the evening

news pulls a flood
of ink from every
pen on earth.

TO BE OPENED AFTER MY DEATH

I saw the plurals rise, I said
I saw the plurals rise

        to describe them   as you see them
        hovering above the toll-

measures

hand through drawer, small pieces of
splinter go

      where the leg goes
widespread

to drape the

      swum-to tower.

No door   on the chorus

she is
bricked^{silked} behind a tower

      holding dank
      strands of grass by the thousand,

minutes of trial time

  under hand

     below hedge space

"in the window in
      the shape of a face."

Far off in a stone meadow

I was run in the gut by a ghost then

    bandaged by

        the shucked petals of your mother's
        plea.

Please metal-coat all yells
  & I will try to bore

    a vacuum of sun-form for

        buoyancy,   the gentlest sight

to see after
collapse

      flat on back.

                    Six-foot-five creatures

      howl from quartz

"an X meeting four diamonds' limbs."

The garage burned. I find your cheek staring after

quartz eyes to rewind your

staring through.

A diamond is a
shower me with reasons

meeting two Xs meeting two Xs meeting.

As for love, his clothes met

        dog scent
        the night
        she won't remember

after shrill I miss
you plunge

grass is realer under a baby's foot &

keens.

Later I light my porch on fire and the hammock goes up.

Sweep from the center of the eye

sweep PLURALS plurals from the epi
center of the eye

                                        skeletons in new polish
                                        we sleep whole cell and
                                        muscle

                                        in a hole in the loud
                                        heartbeat

Dear cinema hair,

    I see

        slow water motions,
          pooled muscle
            at sea-level.

            Is your rose boat made of swan or of
                favorite shirts soaked with whiskey?

            A mother plucks white flowers six hours
            hidden in the river

                    & when

            it slips petal by
            petal off
            she sails.

OBSERVANCE

Babies dressed in deer hooves
shriek through early May

when a house
at any given moment

bleeds hot dryer steam.
Do eyes cue the idea

that people are bones
loaded with cartoon bulk

& angels are cartoon bulk
subtracted from the biggest

of the bones? Bird toes trail
picnic food. To never know what

day it is is
not a bad thing.

The ashtray fills while the not-
circle sucks voices from echoes

& recycles them into less pretty
forms of deafness.

OR NO BLOSSOMS WHERE FRUIT FELL

Afterglow
exploding in the distance,

she hears a peach
molding in the distance.

Bathed by a velvety
mitten of red,

the backside of the grove
is a velvet hell

her head doesn't seem
to know.

Handfuls of moss
lose human features

to darkness, the twin
ghost formerly clasping

gunfire's affect on
the voices of geese.

Knees do not unbend
as the mask thickens

in a pile of black streaks that
burn her lip

and spill to the dark throat
blocked by

her body,
the small lip of the city.

SOME SOULS ARE MADE FOR SWIMMING

Your shoulders
are apples
to bite, love,

to bite the smells of.

These rumbles & agonies
rumble & agonize

a man-shaped form as it
wrenches

divorce from the
stranger's nap.

Her whole drunk body

on the portico steps.

Pulped

rice paper,
cigarillo kiss,

they rehearse half the
boat crash

eleven more times:

1. breath stroke

2. cuddle

3. sing

about the green
lights
below skin.

THIS IS NOT A CENTURY FOR PARADISE

Running is a fall from
palms on the arm of thicker

airs, not a paradise bearing
revisions of time on the blur
accentuating its cuffs. This

decides you, is left to the
islands of dust gathering
secretly in your throat. This

eats you while it hums.

GIFT

Fight the
avalanche
as it
becomes
your
tailgater.

INSIDE THE SHALLOWS

Skull in the cradle of a
lap, a valentine arm
appears quietly in June.

Together on the table
in two identical base-
ments, the fevers of cold

fever sense lull.

MATERIALIQUE

Judging from
the surface,

sharks had begun
to see a cloud

that evaporated years
ago.

With rat's voice
the hollow log talks.

No

I didn't open my
eyes to prove it.

Today the
sun.

Today the
memory of

dividing
your name

into six pieces
and stirring it

into seven
bowls of milk.

The devil girl
develops

an auburn
hairdo.

She must
truly be

a devil girl.

Silhouettes
on each
brick,

tiny people
in the mortar

interlock
for warmth.

IF IT APPEARS SCULPTED

Original carving
brick by brick

of hard stone. So
after the white bed

produces relief in intaglio,
the round comes.

In modern use, branches
hold birds & cats

by fashioning

a plastic substance
out of leftover blood

& cheap romance books,
or by making a mould

for casting metal
to the row of devils.

CACTUS MAN

Centuries ago
the cactus
man ate all fisher-
man booty.

Catching
fish was
torture for
patient

understudies
left with
only sharp
bones.

P.S. Before

men left
the docks, they
attentively
daubed each

other's
noses
& other
weeping parts.

WE FLY BALLOONS

Follow the line of hot
air on the skyline,

nameless, sweet sweet
dismissal of sandbag

to earth made of nine
million open hands.

The greatest view rusts thin
from sex with cloud after

cloud. Have you tried
ambling over the vapors with

ambling shoes? Cloud shoes?
Cloud shoes are a difficult fit.

Seconds crouch,
invisible below the

outer basket, hungry for
useless wizards & falling

sandbags. Still I will
invite you to the swollen

night, the monochrome rainbow
stuck to its wing.

Notes & Additional Thanks

The following titles are loose extractions from the Selected Writings of Henri Michaux (Trans. Richard Ellmann): "This is Not a Century for Paradise," "Some Souls are Made for Swimming," and "You Will Build a City Out of Rags."

Thank you to the following people who helped propel this book to completion: Joshua Marie Wilkinson, Bin Ramke, Eleni Sikelianos, Christina Mengert, Greg Howard, Paul Fattaruso, & the editors of the journals in which some of these poems first appeared. Additional thanks to: Elizabeth Robinson, Liz Cross, Matthew Goulish, Sarah Keller, Brian Kiteley, Laurie White, Arcana, & Sparrow.

Julie Doxsee holds a PhD in English and Creative Writing from the University of Denver, and an MFA in Writing from the School of the Art Institute of Chicago. She was born in London, Ontario in the seventies and has roamed widely since then. Currently she lives and teaches in Istanbul, Turkey.